The
HEART of a
LEADER

INSIGHTS ON THE
ART OF INFLUENCE

KEN
BLANCHARD

transforming lives together

INTRODUCTION

When I was in high school, I had a football coach who loved motivational sayings; he covered the walls of our locker room with them. Sayings like, "When the going gets tough, the tough get going" and "Quitters never win, and winners never quit" were imprinted in my mind. When I started teaching and writing in the field of leadership and management, it was second nature for me to use sayings to help people remember key points. That's why I was thrilled when David C. Cook asked me to update *The Heart of a Leader*, a book that includes my favorite sayings.

Leadership isn't just about having a powerful position. Anytime you use your influence to affect the thoughts and actions of others, you are engaging in leadership. So you can be a leader as a parent, spouse, friend, or citizen. I hope these sayings will give you the wisdom and inspiration you need to lead at a higher level. Remember, the best leaders are those who understand that their power flows through them, not from them.

God bless!

—Ken Blanchard

The key to developing people is to catch them doing something right.

—Ken Blanchard and Spencer Johnson
The One Minute Manager®

Catching people doing things right is a powerful management concept. Unfortunately, most leaders have a genius for catching people doing things wrong. I always recommend that leaders spend at least an hour a week wandering around their operation catching people doing things right. But I remind them that effective praising must be specific. Just walking around saying, "Thanks for everything," is meaningless. If you say, "Great job!" to a poor performer and, "Great job!" to a good performer, you sound ridiculous to the poor performer and you "demotivate" the good performer.

Catching people doing things right provides satisfaction and motivates good performance. But remember, give praise immediately, make it specific, and finally, encourage people to keep up the good work. This principle can also help you shine at home. It's a marvelous way to interact with and affirm the people in your life.

Don't wait until people do things exactly right before you praise them.

—Ken Blanchard and Spencer Johnson
The One Minute Manager

Many well-intentioned leaders wait to praise their people until they do things exactly right, complete the project, or accomplish the goal. The problem here is that they could wait forever. You see, "exactly right" behavior is made up of a whole series of *approximately* right behaviors. It makes more sense to praise progress—it's a moving target.

Can you imagine standing a child up and commanding him to walk, and then, when he falls down, yelling, "I told you to walk!" and spanking him? Of course not. You stand the child up, and he wobbles a bit. You shout, "You stood up!" and then shower him with hugs and kisses. The next day, he wobbles a step, and you are all over him with praise. Gradually, the child gains confidence until he finally walks. It's the same with adults. Catch them doing things right—and remember, in the beginning, approximately right is just fine.

What we give our attention to, grows.

—Ken Blanchard, Thad Lacinak,
Chuck Tompkins, and Jim Ballard
Whale Done!™

The more attention you pay to a behavior, the more it will be repeated. Accentuating the positive and redirecting the negative are the best tools for increasing productivity.

Killer-whale trainers know that when you don't pay a lot of attention to what the animals do wrong but instead give a lot of attention to what they do right, they do the right thing more often. When trainers start working with a new whale, the whale knows nothing about jumping over ropes. The trainers begin with the rope underneath the water, high enough from the bottom for the whale to swim under. If the whale swims under the rope, the trainers don't pay attention, but every time he swims over the rope, they feed him.

Focusing on the negative often creates situations that demoralize people. When good performance is followed by a positive response, people naturally want to continue that behavior.

You get from people
what you expect.

Whenever I talk about the power of catching people doing things right, I hear, "Yeah right. You don't know Harry!" Do you have a "Harry" in your life? If so, perhaps you should take a look at your expectations for that person and see if he or she isn't currently living down to them. It's all in what you notice. When you judge someone, it impairs your ability to see him or her clearly, as if a filter is screening out everything about that person except what fits your assessment.

Fight through your filter and catch your "Harry" doing something right. It will not be easy, but if you persevere, you will notice that your behavior, even your attitude or degree of acceptance toward "Harry" will change. Try it and see what happens. Then try it again. You might even like it. Guaranteed—"Harry" will.

People who produce
good results feel good
about themselves.

—Ken Blanchard and Robert Lorber
Putting the One Minute Manager to Work

In *The One Minute Manager*, Spencer Johnson and I wrote, "People who feel good about themselves produce good results." After the book came out, I realized I was emphasizing the "old" human relations game—trying first to make people feel good, hoping they would then produce good results. Hence Robert Lorber and I changed the emphasis when we wrote *Putting the One Minute Manager to Work*. These days, everything our company does is focused on helping people produce good results.

When people produce good results, they feel good about themselves because they know they have done a good job, and they have something to show for their effort. An effective leader will make it a priority to help his or her people produce good results in two ways: making sure people know what their goals are and doing everything possible to support, encourage, and coach them to accomplish those goals.

Your role as a leader is even more important than you might imagine. You have the power to help people become winners.

Feedback is the breakfast of champions.

—Rick Tate
leadership expert and author

In my travels, I've seen a lot of unmotivated people at work, but I've never seen an unmotivated person after work. When five o'clock rolls around, people race from the office to play golf or tennis, coach Little League, and pursue other pastimes. People are motivated to do things that provide them with feedback on results. Feedback is important to people. We all want to know how well we're doing. That's why it is essential for an effective performance review system to provide ongoing feedback.

Too often managers save up negative information and unload it all at once after a minor incident or during the annual performance review session. Others "whitewash" performance reviews and act like everything is OK when it really isn't. When people are attacked or not dealt with truthfully, they lose respect for their organization and pride in their work.

I firmly believe that providing feedback is the most cost-effective strategy for improving performance and instilling satisfaction. It can be done quickly, it costs nothing, and it can turn people around fast.

No one can make you
feel inferior without
your permission.

—Eleanor Roosevelt

I go out into the world every day with the attitude that my "OKness" is not up for grabs. I firmly believe that "God did not make junk." This doesn't mean I don't have areas of my life that need improvement—but at my basic core, I'm OK. I choose to feel good about myself. That way I am more open to learning. If people give me negative feedback or criticize something I do, I don't interpret what they are saying as meaning that I am a "bad" person. The belief that I control my own self-esteem permits me to listen to and hear their feedback in a nondefensive way—looking to see if there is something I can learn.

Norman Vincent Peale, the great minister of positive thinking, taught me that we have two choices every day: We can feel good about ourselves, or we can feel lousy about ourselves. Why would anyone choose the latter?

It never hurts to toot your
own horn once in a while.

—Ken Blanchard, Thad Lacinak,
Chuck Tompkins, and Jim Ballard
Whale Done!

It's been said that if you don't toot your own horn, someone will come along and use it as a spittoon.

As long as you're busy accentuating the positive in others, a little self-praise doesn't hurt. A lot of managers are hard on others because they're so hard on themselves. They're always thinking, "Oh, I should have done that better," or "What a dummy I am, forgetting that detail." Sound like anybody you know?

If you catch yourself doing things right, everything in your life will improve—especially your relationships. That's because it's fun to be around people who like themselves.

No one of us is as smart as all of us.

—Ken Blanchard, Don Carew, and Eunice Parisi-Carew
The One Minute Manager Builds High Performing Teams

This quote has become the guiding principle of our team-building work in organizations. When I first caught the truth of this statement, it made me relax tremendously as a leader. I realized that I didn't have to be the only bright person in the group. In fact, admitting my vulnerability allowed me to ask for help. I experienced an example of this while working with a large southern manufacturing plant.

The president was baffled by a 200 percent turnover in one of the plant's major hourly positions. I asked to speak to the workers in the affected area, knowing they would be the key to finding an answer.

They told me, "It's hot as the devil down here. We're so exhausted by the end of the day that we don't have energy to do anything else. So if we can get another job, we do." I reported my findings to the president, they fixed the cooling system, and turnover dropped to around 10 percent. By involving the resources we have gathered around us, any problem can be solved.

Get your ego out of the
way and move on.

—Ken Blanchard, Sheldon Bowles,
Don Carew, and Eunice Parisi-Carew
High Five!

The minute you decide to be part of a team, you're going to lose some things and gain others. What you're going to gain is synergy—one plus one equals more than two. What you're going to lose is having your ideas automatically accepted.

If you're going to be part of a winning team, you have to be willing to accept some losses. Certainly fight for your ideas. Try to convince others. But if they can't or won't buy into your thinking, it's time to take a deep breath and let go.

Learning to let go, to put the team's will first, is an empowering experience that leads to the most wonderful of all experiences: being a member of a high-performing, gung-ho, high-five team.

Remember, leadership is not all about you.

Things not worth doing are not worth doing well.

—Ken Blanchard, William Oncken, and Hal Burrows
The One Minute Manager Meets the Monkey

William Oncken Jr., originator of the "monkey-on-the-back" concept, used to say this all the time. For years, time-management experts taught efficiency in all things. Eventually, Oncken and others realized that it didn't make sense for people to be efficient at doing tasks that they shouldn't be doing in the first place.

Today people are often busy doing what seems to be extremely urgent but really isn't. They spend a great deal of time moving paper rather than listening to their people or their customers. An effective leader must step back, look at the big picture, and make sure the important things are not being pushed out of the way by the seemingly urgent needs of the moment.

If your people and customers are important, then you will spend part of every day making them feel that way. Evaluate each day by asking yourself, "Have I done what is really important today?"

Success is not forever and
failure isn't fatal.

—Ken Blanchard and Don Shula
Everyone's a Coach

This was Don Shula's favorite quote when he was the head coach of the Miami Dolphins. It drove a great deal of his behavior during his long and distinguished career as the winningest coach in the history of the NFL.

Don had a twenty-four hour rule. He allowed himself, his coaches, and his players a maximum of twenty-four hours after a football game to celebrate a victory or bemoan a defeat. During that time, they were encouraged to experience the thrill of victory or the agony of defeat as deeply as possible. Once the twenty-four-hour deadline had passed, they put it behind them and focused their energies on preparing for the next opponent. This is a principle well worth noting.

Don't get a big head when you win or get too down in the dumps when you lose. Keep things in perspective. Success is not forever and failure isn't fatal.

Never punish a learner.

—Ken Blanchard and Spencer Johnson
The One Minute Manager

A friend of mine called me about house-training his new dog. "When he has an accident on the rug," he told me, "I plan to shove his nose in it, pound him on the butt with a newspaper, and throw him out the kitchen window into the backyard. How do you think that will work?"

I laughed because I knew exactly what would happen. After three days of this treatment, the dog would poop on the floor and jump out the window! That's the kind of confusion you will get when you use punishment on a learner who lacks confidence or may not fully understand what you expect from him or her. I suggest redirection.

When a learner makes a mistake, be sure he or she knows immediately that the behavior was incorrect. Place the blame on yourself by saying, "Sorry, I didn't make it clear." Then patiently redirect by reviewing the assignment. If possible, demonstrate what a good job looks like. Observe the learner's new behavior in hopes of catching him or her doing something approximately right, and having the opportunity to praise progress.

When you stop learning,

you stop growing.

When I first met Norman Vincent Peale, he was eighty-six years old. What most amazed me about him was that he was excited about every single day. Why? He couldn't wait to find out what he might learn. He often said, "When I stop learning, I might as well lie down because I will be dead." He was learning right up until his death a few years ago on Christmas Eve at age ninety-five.

Learning is more important today than ever before. In the past if a person was loyal and worked hard, his or her job was secure. Today, the skills you bring to the party constitute the only available form of job security. People who are continually learning and upgrading their skills increase their value in their specific organizations and the job market in general.

The only three things we can count on are death, taxes, and change. Since organizations are being bombarded with change, you would be wise to make learning a top priority and constantly strive to adapt to new circumstances.

When you stop learning,
you stop leading.

—Ken Blanchard and Mark Miller
The Secret

The very best leaders are learners—people who are always interested in ways to enhance their own knowledge and skills. Great leaders find their own approach to learning. Some read, some listen to tapes, some spend time with mentors. They do whatever it takes to keep learning.

Some people might think that once you know how to do your job, you can devote your time and attention to more important matters than ongoing learning. But as a leader, you must model the behavior you want others to emulate. If you're not serious about learning, you can bet the majority of those watching you won't be either.

By continuing to learn, you can keep up with the competition, respond to new challenges, and maximize your God-given talents.

Leadership is a high calling.

—Ken Blanchard
Leading at a Higher Level

Leadership should not be done purely for personal gain or goal accomplishment; it should fulfill a much higher purpose. Nothing is wrong with accomplishing goals, but when you focus solely on results, you miss the big picture. As a result, things like morale and job satisfaction will tend to fall by the wayside. Leadership becomes about getting as much as you can for as little effort as possible. With that kind of leadership, it's a short leap to thinking that the only reason to be in business is to make money. Leaders are forced to choose between people and results because they falsely believe that they can't focus on both at the same time.

Leading at a higher level is the process of achieving worthwhile results while acting with respect, care, and fairness for the well-being of all involved. It's only when you realize that it's not about you that you begin to lead at a higher level.

In life, what you
resist, persists.

—Werner Erhard
founder of "est Training"

If something is bothering you and you don't deal with it, you are gunnysacking your feelings—holding them inside. This can backfire later when you find yourself "dumping" in an inappropriate way and at exactly the wrong moment. Most of the time, if you simply deal with what is bothering you, the problem will disappear in the process. Have you ever said, "I'm glad I got that off my mind"?

Years ago, I worked for several divisions of AT&T during the transition to seven sister companies. Though top leadership emphasized the benefits of the change, associates were not being encouraged to deal with their feelings. I set up venting sessions where they could "mourn" their personal losses as companies were restructured. The associates were urged to share their feelings of loss regarding status, lifetime employment, and similar frustrations. Soon, they became much more open to hearing about the benefits of the changes and were able to move forward with their lives and careers.

As Yogi Berra said, "It felt like déjà vu all over again" lately when I recommended mourning sessions to help Bell South associates deal with their recent takeover by AT&T.

What you resist, persists. Until you deal with your feelings, you will be stuck with them.

Don't work harder—
work smarter.

This concept is common sense but not common practice. Most people still think there is a direct relationship between the amount of work they do and their success—the more time they put in, the more successful they will be. When asked to speak to a group of college students about what it takes to be successful, one accomplished entrepreneur said, "This will be the shortest speech in history because it's easy to be successful. All you have to do is work half a day. You can work the first twelve hours or the second."

Successful people do work hard, but they also think before they act. They are proactive, not just reactive. Most people mentally have a sign on their desk that reads, "Don't just sit there—do something!" The best advice I ever received was to revise the sign to read, "Don't just do something—sit there!"

If you don't take time out to think, strategize, and prioritize, you will work a whole lot harder, without enjoying the benefits of a job smartly done.

Nice guys may appear
to finish last, but usually
they are running in a
different race.

—Ken Blanchard and Norman Vincent Peale
The Power of Ethical Management

People today want what they want, and they want it right now. A negative side effect of such impatience is poor decision-making. Patience helps us realize that if we do what is right—even if it costs us in the short run—it will pay off in the long run.

Norman Vincent Peale told a story about a nice guy who eventually won. The man was fired as the art director of a magazine because he refused to work on a project that included what he considered to be pornographic material. He had a difficult time finding another job, and even his kids had to get after-school jobs to help out.

Finally, almost a year later, he was offered a great job—even better than the one he had lost. Ironically, he clinched the new job as a result of his old boss's recommendation! He had earned his boss's respect. The man's patience paid off because he was running in a different race.

In managing people, it
is easier to loosen up
than tighten up.

—Ken Blanchard, Patricia Zigarmi, and Drea Zigarmi
Leadership and The One Minute Manager

If you are not sure how much direction people need when working on a task, it's always better to oversupervise than undersupervise in the beginning. Why? Because if you find that your people are better performers than you thought, and you loosen up, they will like you and respond in a positive way. It also helps as you seek to communicate your growing respect for the quality of work they are producing.

On the other hand, if you start off undersupervising your people and later discover that their skills are not as good as you had anticipated, you then have a sticky situation. Even when it is appropriate to correct or redirect their work, you may find that they perceive your efforts as undue criticism, micromanaging, or even persecution. After all, they aren't doing anything differently, so why are you suddenly bent on changing things? Resentment grows.

Remember: it's always easier to loosen up than to tighten up.

Anything worth doing
does not have to be done
perfectly—at first.

Managers should recognize that good performance— both their own and their people's—is a journey, not an announced destination. Everyone learns by doing. It takes time and practice to achieve specific goals.

For example, the managers who attend my training seminars often get very excited by some of the concepts they learn. They return to their organizations all fired up about using a new idea or approach. However, when people don't respond immediately as anticipated, these managers often become discouraged and abandon the concept, deciding that it doesn't work.

Being too hard on yourself is counterproductive. Don't expect instant perfection. Though self-criticism is healthy, it should not be destructive. It's unfair to be hard on yourself the first time you attempt something new. It is also unfair to expect others to meet such an unrealistic expectation. Keep in mind that it's unnecessary to do everything exactly right the first time.

What motivates people is
what motivates people.

Motivation is a difficult concept for most leaders. Many assume that money, prizes, or special vacations are high-grade motivators. In reality, what motivates one person may not motivate another.

Suppose you have two excellent people. You would like to reward one with a raise in pay, but money, it turns out, is not an issue with this person since his or her spouse has a good job that provides a sufficient second income. He or she may see increased responsibility as an appropriate reward. On the other hand, you would like to reward the second person with more responsibility, but his or her spouse's unexpected illness has created big medical bills. For this person, money is a greater motivator than increased responsibility.

How do you know which type of motivation works with different people? Ask! Try something like, "If you perform well, what kind of reward or recognition could you receive that would make you want to continue to perform at a high level?" It pays to ask this important question.

Life is all about getting As.

During my ten years of teaching at a college, my fellow faculty members occasionally reprimanded me because I always gave out the final examination questions on the first day of class. When my colleagues asked why I did this, I would reply, "Because I plan to spend the semester teaching them the answers so when it comes time for the final, everyone will get an A."

My teaching example parallels the three parts of an effective review system: performance planning when goals and objectives are set, day-to-day coaching when ongoing feedback is given, and performance evaluation when overall performance is determined.

In business, communicating performance objectives—giving people the final exam questions ahead of time—is the perfect way to ensure that everyone is working from the same sheet of music and headed in the right direction. Once goals are clear, leaders should wander around and "teach people the answers" so when they take the final exam, they will get As. After all, that's what life is all about!

Create Raving Fans; satisfied customers are not good enough.

—Ken Blanchard and Sheldon Bowles
Raving Fans®

What are Raving Fan customers? These are customers who are so happy about the way you treated them that they want to brag about you. In essence, they become part of your sales force.

There is a lot of competition out there. If you don't take care of your customers, somebody else is ready to take your place. Let's face it—you may not get a second chance. In fact, alienating customers can earn you a reputation for non-service that can stymie the best sales team and most savvy advertising campaign.

Differentiate yourself from your competition by teaching your sales force and customer-service representatives—everyone who comes in contact with your public—to develop Raving Fan customers. Going the extra mile for the people who write your checks will pay off.

If you want to know why
your people are not
performing well, step up to
the mirror and take a peek.

From my point of view, one of the worst concepts in the history of leadership theory is the "Peter Principle." According to the Peter Principle, people in organizations tend to rise to their level of incompetence. In other words, they keep getting promoted until they become a failure. I believe this concept lets managers off the hook.

Good leaders are committed to helping their people win. When someone fails, they accept responsibility for that failure. I think anytime you fire someone who works for you, or anytime you're looking for a place to hide someone who works for you (Lawrence Peter called this "a lateral arabesque"), you should step up to a mirror and take a peek. In most cases, the biggest cause of the problem will be looking you in the eyes.

The main job of a leader is to help his or her people succeed in accomplishing their goals. And when people accomplish their goals and win, everyone wins.

Managing only for profit is like playing tennis with your eye on the scoreboard and not on the ball.

—Ichak Adizes
corporate performance expert and author

The best definition of *profit* I've ever heard is that it is the applause you get for satisfying your customers and creating a motivating environment for your people. Too bad Wall Street doesn't embrace that definition. The problem is that too many people act like the only reason to stay in business is to make money. Their eyes are on the scoreboard rather than the ball!

Successful organizations today have a triple bottom line—very much like a three-legged stool. The three legs of the stool are Raving Fan customers, gung ho people, and financial strength. All three legs have to be strong for the stool to stand. If you focus on only one leg, the stool will fall. Even if you focus on two legs, but forget the third, the stool will still fall.

And if you focus only on financial success and forget about your people and your customers, eventually, your financial success will decline.

If you want your people to be responsible, be responsive to their needs.

—Ken Blanchard, Bill Hybels, and Phil Hodges
Leadership by the Book

The traditional hierarchy is OK for goal setting. People look to the head of their department and to the top of their organization for direction. But once goals are clear, the pyramid should, in essence, be turned upside down. This way, the customers are at the top of the hierarchy, followed by the customer-contact people, while the president and the chair of the board are at the bottom.

When this philosophy is implemented, your role as a leader changes from being *responsible* to being *responsive*. Your job becomes to work with your people, rather than having them work for you. Being responsive to your people's needs sets them free to be responsible (able to respond) for getting the job done.

Make your people responsible for doing high-quality work by responding to their needs and supporting them. That places the responsibility at the appropriate level—with the people who do the work.

It's more important as a manager to be respected than to be popular.

—Ken Blanchard and Don Shula
Everyone's a Coach

Think back to a leader you had—a parent, teacher, coach, or boss—who got great performance from you. More than likely, this was a leader who combined being tough with being nice. You knew that person cared about you, but you also knew that he or she would not let up on you in the quest for excellence.

If you, as a leader, demand that your people add value to the organization through their work, you must fulfill your end of the bargain by telling the truth and keeping work standards high. This often means sacrificing popularity in your endeavor to do the right thing.

Are you willing to push your people—whether it's a group of middle managers or a Cub Scout pack—beyond their comfort zone in order to achieve excellence? They might not like what you ask of them, but they will remember you as a leader they respected.

People with humility don't think less of themselves, they just think of themselves less.

—Ken Blanchard and Norman Vincent Peale
The Power of Ethical Management

A friend of mine jokes about his latest book, *Humility and How I Attained It*. It reminds me of what I call the greatest addiction in the world today—the human ego. Leaders who fall victim to this addiction want to be center stage. Often, they are threatened by the successes of others, so they fail to develop and use people's talents or catch them doing something right. These leaders want to be the best— "the fairest of them all."

Here's a great rule for doing business today: Think more about your people, and they will think more of themselves. And don't act like you are perfect. Leaders need to come out from behind their curtains of infallibility, power, and control, and let their "very good" side—their humanity—be revealed. Folks like to be around people who are willing to admit their vulnerability, ask for ideas, and can let others be in the spotlight.

Never give in!
Never give in!
Never give in!
Never!

—Winston Churchill

On October 29, 1949, Winston Churchill gave one of his most famous speeches at Harrow, the English prep school he attended as a boy. Rumor had it that on that day Churchill stood up, gave a three-word speech—"Never give in!"—and sat down.

While that story is not entirely true—Churchill delivered a longer speech that day—it's absolutely true that it became one of his most celebrated speeches.

If one quality epitomized Winston Churchill, it was persistence. He never gave up. It was that attitude that inspired England in World War II to continue fighting when others might have surrendered.

Persistence means sticking to your guns. It's keeping your commitment and making your actions consistent with your word. It's all about "walking your talk."

Trying is just a noisy way
of not doing something.

I learned from author and consultant Art Turock that we need to make a distinction between being interested and being committed. When you are interested in doing something, you only do it when it's convenient, but when you are committed, you follow through no matter what—no excuses!

Many people are interested, rather than committed. They talk about trying to do something, rather than actually doing it. They make lots of noise but fail to follow up. An interested exerciser wakes up in the morning to rain and says, "I think I'll exercise tomorrow." A committed exerciser wakes up to rain and says, "I better exercise inside."

When a person is committed to doing something, he or she will find ways to suppress rationalization. Even when it is inconvenient, such a person will keep his or her commitment. Persistence in life is characterized by this mental and behavioral toughness.

Good thoughts in
your head that are
not communicated
mean "squat."

There are three responses people can receive from leadership concerning their performance—positive, negative, or no response at all. Only one response of the three tends to increase good performance—the positive one. And yet, the major leadership style used today is to say nothing at all.

A person who does something correctly and receives a positive response will most likely continue that desired behavior in the future. By the same token, a person who receives a negative response for doing something wrong will most likely not repeat the behavior. But what if that same person does something correctly and receives no response at all? The behavior may continue for a while, but eventually it will decline. Why? Because no one seems to care.

Many leaders notice their people doing things right and think well of them. Unfortunately, they do not always put those positive thoughts into words. As a result, this good performance gets no response. If you want to get and maintain good performance, you must let your people know you notice and care about the things they do right. Share your good thoughts.

You may fool the
whole world down the
pathway of life,

And get pats on your
back as you pass,

But your final reward will
be heartaches and tears

If you've cheated the
man in the glass.

—Dale Wimbrow
writer

This is the closing verse of a poem given to Norman Vincent Peale by Lowell Thomas one day after hearing one of Norman's sermons. Thomas said to him, "Frankly, if you had read this poem, your talk would have been much better." Obviously Dr. Peale agreed, because he kept a copy of the poem in his wallet and referred to it frequently.

While the message is loud and clear, you might ask, "But don't some people do the wrong thing and then rationalize what they've done?" Yes, people do that, but if they take a good hard look at themselves, down deep they know they have done wrong.

You can't go against the image you have of yourself and your opinion about what you think is right without feeling bad. It's counter to your purpose—the picture you have of yourself as an ethical person. A clear purpose is the foundation upon which sound, ethical behavior is built.

Sometimes when the numbers look right, the decision is still wrong!

—Ken Blanchard and Norman Vincent Peale
The Power of Ethical Management

G ood business requires more than simply calculating which choice will make the most money. It requires developing a way to step back from a situation and put it in perspective.

I know a leader who uses a three-step approach when faced with a serious problem or an important decision. First, he calls his team together for information gathering. Each person is asked to contribute until as much information as possible has been amassed about the problem or decision. Second, the group works together to word what he calls "the right question." If answered, this question should yield the best possible solution. Third, he asks each person to sit quietly for ten minutes and look for the answer within. He calls this "inward listening."

My friend has been amazed by the clarity of thought and agreement that emerges from these sessions. If you don't find creative ways like this to put things in perspective, you will continue to be driven only by the bottom line.

Love is being able to say you're sorry.

—Ken Blanchard and Margret McBride
The Fourth Secret (formerly *The One Minute Apology*)

Even if you didn't read Eric Segal's book *Love Story* or see the movie, I'll bet you can recall the story's famous line, "Love is never having to say you're sorry." People loved that statement, but I think it's awful, especially for leaders. I think it should read, "Love is being able to say you're sorry." But saying "I'm sorry" is tough on the ego. Leaders are often reluctant to admit they are wrong and ask forgiveness.

Some years ago, I received a letter from a top manager at Honeywell who suggested that the fourth secret of *The One Minute Manager* should be the "One Minute Apology." That resonated with me because my mother always said, "There are two statements that people don't use enough that could change the world: "thank you" and "I'm sorry." The "One Minute Praising" covered "thank you," but we didn't have anything that corresponded to "I'm sorry."

If you, as a leader, can give up being right and learn to apologize for your mistakes, your organization will be a lot better place for people to work. Thanks, Mom.

Without a change in your behavior, just saying, "I'm sorry" is not enough.

—Ken Blanchard and Margret McBride
The Fourth Secret (formerly *The One Minute Apology*)

It's human to make mistakes. When leaders mess up (after all, leaders are only human), the One Minute Apology is one of the most powerful things they can do. If leaders don't learn to apologize and repair the problems they've created by their mistakes, they lose the confidence of their bosses and coworkers.

Saying "I'm sorry" is just the first step in an effective apology. The only way you can demonstrate that you are really sorry is by changing your behavior. When you do this, the people you have harmed know that you are committed to not repeating the mistake. The longer you wait to apologize, the sooner your weakness will be perceived as wickedness.

The power of the One Minute Apology is deeper than just saying a few words: It's an investment in relationships that reaps countless rewards.

Good religion is like
good football; it isn't
talk, it's action.

—Ken Blanchard and Don Shula
Everyone's a Coach

P eople in general, and especially those in the business world, are looking for leaders whose faith works for them on a day-to-day basis. Why? Because in business today, opponents are multiplying, risks are increasing, and the number of factors that could spell success or failure is proliferating constantly.

To win this new business game, your faith must be the genuine article. You must be able to rely on intuition—that calm inner voice that tells you what to do. At the same time, you must be relentless in your pursuit of opportunity. This paradoxical equilibrium between trusting in your own way as you approach danger and calmly discerning the outward signals is actually very close to what we call "faith."

Traditionally, business and religion have been seen as opposite approaches. That day is over. The demands of business and of life are too great. Thank God!

Take what you do seriously
but yourself lightly.

—Ken Blanchard and Terry Waghorn
Mission Possible

A tendency toward grimness and seriousness can stifle an organization's environment and limit its creativity. You can tell right away when you visit a company where no one is having any fun—people look like they are running around with tight underwear on. They are longing to lighten up, but they have no permission.

These days, leaders and managers are being offered courses in humor. These classes don't teach the art of telling a good joke. Instead, they are aimed at helping people contact something they already have inside—their sense of humor. Increasing someone's natural ability to see the funny or absurd side of a situation will have a direct bearing on his or her effectiveness with others.

Today's leaders must relearn the value of a smile or they will be unable to fire up the ability of their people to find real enjoyment in their work. So start thinking smiles until you become a smile millionaire. People will be glad to see you coming.

Character is following through on decisions.

—Ken Blanchard, Jim Ballard, and Fred Finch
Customer Mania!

A lot of people love to make announcements—yet it's commitments, not announcements, that really matter. Commitment involves making sure that what you intend to do or what you announce you will do actually gets done. "The road to hell is paved with good intentions." It's an old, but true, saying. How do you overcome that? Put some structure around your good intentions.

For example, I'm sure you know people who are very thoughtful. They always remember your birthday. How do they do that? They have a system in their organizers or Palm Pilots so that a week to ten days before your birthday, up pops information that ignites their good intention to remember your birthday. Effective leadership is like that: It requires creating systems that will help you to follow up on your good decisions.

The trouble with being
in a rat race is that even
if you win the race,
you're still a rat.

—Lily Tomlin
actress and comedian

W e all have two selves—an inner self that is thoughtful, reflective, and a good listener; and an outer, task-oriented self. Our inner self is focused on connecting with people and finding significance in life, while our outer, task-oriented self is focused on achieving and is often too busy to learn.

To avoid the rat race and stay on course, we must honor our inner selves. The only way to do that is to seek out times of solitude, when we can be alone with the voice that says, "You are a loved and valuable person."

Solitude is hard to find. Therefore, I recommend that people enter their day slowly by engaging in an activity that is intrinsically valuable and noncompetitive, such as prayer, meditation, reflective reading, or certain kinds of exercise that allow for reflection, such as walking, jogging, swimming, or biking.

The cure for too much to do is solitude and silence.

—Ken Blanchard and Phil Hodges
The Servant Leader

S olitude and silence give us some space to reform our innermost attitudes toward people and events. For a brief time, they take the weight of the world off our shoulders and interrupt our habit of constantly managing things and of being in control—or at least thinking we are.

In solitude and silence, we find that we are safely more than what we do and that we are never truly alone.

Find someplace where you can be totally out of contact with all kinds of human noise (television, cell phone, fax machine, voicemail, that secret pile of paperwork, magazines, even this book) for a minimum of thirty minutes. Place your hands, palms down, on your knees, mentally laying down everything you are concerned about for the day. When you have finished naming your concerns, turn your hands up, ready to receive what God reveals to you. Have no expectations or agenda for this time with God. Let it be His to fill.

Think Big!
Act Big!
Be Big!

—Norman Vincent Peale

At his ninetieth birthday party, Norman Vincent Peale shared a story about a man he met on a plane. The man looked worried so Norman decided to engage him in conversation. "What's wrong?" he asked. After some coaxing, the man shared that he had just received a promotion but had doubts about whether he had what it would take to handle the job.

"Yes you do!" stated Dr. Peale.

"How do you know?" the man replied.

Dr. Peale answered, "You do if you think you do." Then he encouraged the man to start each day by chanting, "Think big! Act big! Be big!" By the time they landed, the man was in a different frame of mind.

Be your own best friend and believe in yourself. Don't wait for someone to do it for you. Cheer yourself on. Write your own pep talk. It works.

Real communication
happens when
people feel safe.

Real communication is a product of trust. However, most of the performance review and evaluation systems used in organizations today create mistrust. They are based on a normal distribution mentality that insists that there must always be winners and losers. That has never made sense to me.

No organization makes a habit of hiring losers! You either hire winners (people you already know are good performers) or potential winners (people you think can become good performers). So why would you ever sort your people out into a normal distribution? Your job is to bring out their magnificence.

Find ways to convince your people that you see them all as either winners or potential winners and that you mean them no harm. When you do, you will find that communication within your organization is greatly enhanced.

Without vision, the people perish.

—Proverbs 29:18 (paraphrased)

L eaders today must have a strong vision and positive beliefs that support that vision. If they don't, their people will not only lose, but they'll be lost. When difficulties arise, their minds will not be prepared to stand up to the challenge.

A clear vision is really just a picture of how things would be if everything were running as planned. The most powerful dream a leader can have is a vision of perfection. Dreams lift us up. If we really believe them, we start acting as if they are already true. That kind of enthusiasm is contagious.

All great companies and teams have a visionary leader at the helm, someone who is always pointing toward the kind of organization they're going to be. People have a need to follow this type of leader, an inspiring individual who keeps them on track when difficulties arise.

Vision is knowing who
you are, where you're
going, and what will
guide your journey.

—Ken Blanchard and Jesse Stoner
Full Steam Ahead!

P eople need vision. During times of growth, change, opportunity, or uncertainty, a vision keeps us heading in the right direction. After all, if we don't know who we are, it really doesn't matter where we are going. And if we're going somewhere, we need to be clear about the values that will guide our journey and help us make the tough decisions when we hit obstacles. It's what allows us to go "full steam ahead."

Collectively and individually, we need a significant purpose, clear values, and a picture that shows us what these elements look like when we are living them consistently. Vision gives meaning to our lives and provides direction. It helps us get focused, remain energized, and produce great results.

Vision is a lot more than putting a plaque on the wall. A real vision is lived, not framed.

—Ken Blanchard and Jesse Stoner
Full Steam Ahead!

I t's one thing to identify your vision. It's another to make it happen. If you're an organizational leader, you can't just go out and announce your new vision and expect everyone to immediately understand it or agree to it. You need to consider who should be involved in shaping the vision and be open to their thoughts, dreams, hopes, and needs. You must be willing to allow them to help shape it.

When a vision is shared, it is important to hold one another accountable for behaving consistently with it. If you ignore the behavior of others who act inconsistently with the vision, you threaten the trust and commitment of people who are making the effort to follow through with the vision.

It takes courage to create a vision, and it takes courage to act on it.

All good performance starts with clear goals.

—Ken Blanchard and Spencer Johnson
The One Minute Manager

The reason Spencer Johnson and I made "One Minute Goal Setting" the first secret of *The One Minute Manager* is that we thought the Cheshire Cat was right. Do you remember the story?

Alice was puzzled. As she searched for a way out of Wonderland, she came to a fork in the road. "Which road should I take?" she asked the Cheshire Cat.

"Where are you going?" the cat inquired.

Alice said she didn't know.

The smiling cat gave her this reply, "If you don't know where you're going, any road will get you there."

An important way to motivate your people is to make sure they know where they are going. See that each person's goals are clearly defined and that he or she knows what it means to perform well. This will give people a clear focus for their energy and put them on the road to becoming high-performing, empowered producers.

Different strokes for different folks.

—Ken Blanchard, Patricia Zigarmi, and Drea Zigarmi
Leadership and The One Minute Manager

For years, people thought that the best leadership style was a "participative" style, which prescribed listening to your people and involving them in decision making. Autocratic leadership, which involves the leader taking control and telling people what to do, was considered inappropriate.

In the 1960s, my friend Paul Hersey and I questioned those assumptions. The problem we found was that asking inexperienced members of a team to participate in decision making amounted to "pooling ignorance." Some people need a "directive" leadership style until their knowledge and skills mature. Our response was to develop a concept called Situational Leadership®, which can be summed up in the phrase "Different strokes for different folks." In the 1980s, Paul Hersey and I decided to go in separate directions in our work. Situational Leadership® II is the model my colleagues and I developed.

So what is the best leadership style? The one that matches the developmental needs of the person with whom you're working.

Different strokes for the same folks.

—Ken Blanchard, Patricia Zigarmi, and Drea Zigarmi
Leadership and the One Minute Manager

Situational Leadership® II is a model that identifies four development levels people go through as they move from dependence to independence in completing a task.

These include the Enthusiastic Beginner (excited but has little knowledge), the Disillusioned Learner (learning the task was tougher than he or she thought), the Capable but Cautious Performer (knows how to do it but is nervous about doing it on his or her own), and the Self-Reliant Achiever (confident, motivated, and has the necessary skills).

The point is that no individual is at any one stage in all the tasks he or she performs. Consequently, the same person may need different leadership styles (different strokes) for various tasks. For example, when I was a college professor, I loved to teach and write. Those were tasks I performed well and without supervision. However, when it came to administrative matters like managing my budget and filling out reports, I was a Disillusioned Learner at best. Sometimes it takes different strokes for the same folks.

If God had wanted us
to talk more than listen,
He would have given
us two mouths rather
than two ears.

—Ken Blanchard
We Are the Beloved

When you ask people about the best leader they ever had, one quality is always mentioned: they are good listeners. These leaders have learned to "sort by others." When someone says, "It's a beautiful day," they respond by keeping the focus on the speaker. For example, they'll respond, "It sounds like you're pretty happy today." Poor listeners "sort by self." If you express a concern you have, they will express a concern they have.

Our senior consulting partner, Laurie Hawkins, is a great listener. Clients tell me, "I had the greatest dinner with Laurie recently. He's a wonderful person." When I ask what they know about Laurie—whether he's married or has kids—they seldom know. They loved being with Laurie because he kept the conversation focused on them.

Test the power of listening by taking time to truly listen and focus on others.

Life is what happens to
you while you're busy
making other plans.

—John Lennon

Observing successful people over the years, I've noticed that they don't let disappointments stop them. When one door closes, they look for another to open.

I went off to Cornell University, intent on getting my degree and becoming a highly paid salesman. All the vocational preference tests verified that path as my best career choice. I applied for a summer sales internship and made the finals, but after extensive interviews, I failed to get the job. At the time, I was serving as a dormitory counselor, so someone encouraged me to get my doctorate and become a dean of students. With my doctoral degree in hand, I applied for many good jobs, but I was turned down because of a lack of experience. Undeterred, I set my sights on becoming a faculty member, but I was told that would be impossible because my writing wasn't academic enough.

"So how," you might ask, "did you become a writer and teacher?" That's a long story, but along the way I learned to live by this rule: Keep your head up, and look for the next opportunity.

If you don't seek
perfection, you can never
reach excellence.

—Ken Blanchard and Don Shula
Everyone's a Coach

The level of people's expectations has a great deal to do with the results they achieve. Don Shula's vision of perfection for the football team he coached was to win every game. Was that possible? No. But the 1972 Miami Dolphins did it for a season, establishing a level of perfection that no other NFL team has ever matched.

Don's philosophy is that if you're shooting at a target, you're better off aiming at the bull's-eye because if you miss it, the chances are high you'll still hit the target. On the other hand, if you aim just for the target and miss, you're nowhere.

If Shula's goal had been just to win more games than he lost, do you think he would have recorded the only perfect season on record and become the winningest coach in NFL history? Personally, I don't think so.

People without
information cannot act
responsibly. People with
information are compelled
to act responsibly.

—Ken Blanchard, John P. Carlos, and Alan Randolph
Empowerment Takes More Than a Minute

Have you ever had the experience of trying to resolve a problem, only to get the runaround? Let's say you were overcharged. The frontline person listens to your problem, asks for documentation, and then you both wait around while the person calls the manager to come and approve your refund. Doesn't this leave you with the impression that the organization doesn't trust its people and the only employees who have brains are the managers?

When people are given detailed information about the impact of costs and are entrusted to make decisions, their self-esteem rises and customer service improves. That's why Ritz-Carlton hotel employees are given a $2,000 discretionary fund to resolve customer complaints. Employees of KFC, Taco Bell, and Pizza Hut are given a $10 discretionary fund—a lot of money in a quick-service restaurant. The point is, people with information are empowered to make responsible decisions and help the organization succeed.

Let people bring their
brains to work, and let
them use their knowledge.

—Ken Blanchard and Jesse Stoner
Leading at a Higher Level

Research has shown that when people are empowered to make decisions and take initiative, the organizations benefit overall. Leaders of the best-run companies know that empowering people creates positive results that are not possible when all of the authority has moved up the hierarchy and managers shoulder all the responsibility for success.

For many leaders, it's hard to change to a mindset that shifts responsibility to their people. We feel it is our responsibility as parents, teachers, or managers to tell people what to do, how to do it, and why it needs to be done. We believe it would be avoiding our responsibility to ask children, students, or direct reports to think about what needs to be done and how they should go about achieving those goals.

Leaders must make a leap of faith and fight the battle against the command-and-control tradition. Empowerment requires a major shift in attitude. The most crucial place where this shift must occur is in the heart of every leader.

There's only power in empowerment if you are a self-leader.

—Ken Blanchard, Susan Fowler and Laurence Hawkins
Self Leadership and The One Minute Manager

I f someone has given you additional responsibility, you need to shift from "waiting to be told" to taking the initiative to lead yourself.

Self-leaders become partners with their leaders. They develop the ability to pick up the ball and run with it. They learn how to challenge their assumed constraints— beliefs that limit them—and reach for what they need to succeed. Self-leaders learn to use all their points of power—knowledge power, task power, personal power, and relationship power—rather than relying only on their position power. Finally, self-leaders learn how to collaborate with others to get the support and direction they need to achieve their goals.

When goals work out, it is usually because you instinctively take the initiative to be a self-leader and get what you need to succeed.

A river without banks is a
large puddle.

—Ken Blanchard, John P. Carlos, and Alan Randolph
Empowerment Takes More Than a Minute

S tart your people on a journey to the land of empowerment, but don't forget that they need boundaries. If you
cut them loose without any direction, they will get lost and
revert back to their old unempowered habits. Like the banks
of a river, boundaries have the ability to channel energy in
the right direction. If you take away the boundaries, your
people will lose their momentum and direction.

Boundaries that create autonomy include:

Purpose—what does your company do?

Values—what are your company's operational guide-
lines?

Goals—where is your company headed?

Roles—who does what?

Structure—how is your company organized?

Don't send inexperienced people off alone and then pun-
ish them when they make mistakes. Establish clear
boundaries that will free them to make decisions, take initiative, act like owners, and stay on track.

Leadership is not just what happens when you're there; it's what happens when you're not there.

—Ken Blanchard and Marc Muchnick
The Leadership Pill

Leading effectively means more than just getting results; it means getting the commitment of the team. Many leaders focus only on results and forget about their people. They bang people over their heads until the job gets done. Their definition of success is the team's short-term output.

The true test of leadership, on the other hand, is to win the trust and respect of the team, keep motivation running high, and help it reach new heights. When you win your team's trust, it will work together and consistently perform well over time—even when you're not around.

Leading people is the opposite of trying to control them; it's about gaining their trust through your integrity, developing their potential through your partnership, and motivating them through your affirmation.

Your game is only as good
as your practice.

—Ken Blanchard and Don Shula
Everyone's a Coach

Coach Don Shula believed in "practice perfection." He often quoted Paul Brown, the legendary coach of the Cleveland Browns, who said, "Football is a game of errors. The team that makes the fewest errors in a game usually wins."

Companies need to approach the performance of their people with the same kind of attention to quality; however, as I travel around looking at organizations, I rarely find this emphasis on "practice perfection." Far more often, companies hire highly competent people, get them started, and then leave them to struggle on their own.

No individual or team can reach "practice perfection" alone. It takes ferocious concentration and unyielding commitment to continuous improvement. That means day-to-day coaching—setting clear goals, letting people perform, observing, and then praising progress or redirecting efforts. Most managers miss the "observing" step. They give directions, but they don't stick around to redirect their people or to catch them doing something right. "You can't coach from the press box," Shula said. "You have to be on the field."

All empowerment exists in
the present moment.

Consider moments when you were at your best, and you will find that you were right there in the moment, fully and completely present. If you dwell only on "what was" or "what will be," you will miss the power of "what is."

Spencer Johnson, coauthor of *The One Minute Manager*, discusses this important truth in his brilliant parable, "The Precious Present." In the story, an older man's wisdom launches a young boy on a lifelong search for the "precious present." Finally, he discovers what the old man was trying to teach him: To learn from the past is good, but to live there is a waste. To plan for the future is good, but to live there is a waste. You are happiest and most productive in life when you are living in the present.

All highly effective leaders have learned to respect the power of the present. They have discovered that analyzing the past and planning for the future is not enough; they must also nurture the present and celebrate its victories.

We are not human beings having a spiritual experience. We are spiritual beings having a human experience.

I t becomes clearer to me all the time that leaders today have to start being cheerleaders, supporters, and encouragers, rather than judges, critics, and evaluators. Unfortunately, it's almost impossible for people to play these new roles if they don't feel good about themselves.

I believe that the quickest and most powerful way for an individual to significantly enhance his or her self-esteem and become a more loving and accepting person is by having a "spiritual awakening."

Suppose we all accepted the fact that we possess the unconditional love of God our Father—that we can't achieve enough, sell enough, build enough, or own enough to merit more love—that we have all the love there is. Would knowing this truth make us better cheerleaders, supporters, and encouragers for our people? I think so. When you discover that you are a spiritual being having a human experience, you realize that everyone else is, too.

I have never seen a
U-Haul attached to
a hearse.

In his book *Ordering Your Private World,* Gordon MacDonald makes the distinction between people who are "driven" and people who are "called." Driven people spend most of their time defending what they own their ideas, relationships, and possessions.

On the other hand, called people live by the philosophy that everything is on loan. They contend that we come into this world with nothing, and we leave with nothing. I agree—with one exception. I think when all is said and done, all we can take with us is the love we feel toward others and the love they have sent our way.

Rabbi Harold Kushner, author of *When Bad Things Happen to Good People,* said: "I've never heard someone on their deathbed say, 'I wish I'd gone to the office more!' They all say something like, 'I wish I'd cared more. I wish I'd loved more. I wish I'd reached out to others more.'" This is both a sobering thought and a call to action.

Perpetual prosperity comes
to those who help others.

—Ken Blanchard and Sheldon Bowles
Big Bucks!

Moneymaking is about what you can get; perpetual prosperity is about what you can give. Success at the money level is about what you can achieve; perpetual prosperity is about how you can serve. There are many good reasons to earn money, but some people seek money because of the power and status it will give them to control events and other people.

While some of us never get beyond money or the things money buy, most of us know a void in our lives needs to be filled if we only pay attention to making money.

When we reach out to help someone else, we often get more back in return. That's not why we help people; that's just how it works sometimes.

Inquire within.

Most of the significant advances in human history—great social and political reformations, artistic productions, and unique inventions—have come not from rushing around, but from being still. They required periods of deep and rigorous contemplation, for only in this way can we escape the clamor of outer voices that remind us of "how we've always done it."

How do we find this time for solitude and introspection? We must stake it out for ourselves. One top manager I know does not allow his people to talk on the phone or meet between 8:30 and 9:30 in the morning. This is their quiet time. I used to talk to people on airplanes. Now I use that time to reflect, read, write, or just quiet my mind. I am amazed by my creativity after a long flight.

The point here is that there is no way to do silence wrong. The only wrong thing would be to not do it.

People in organizations
need to develop a
fascination for what
doesn't work.

When a mistake is made in your organization, what's the first question asked? "What can we learn?" or "Who is to blame?" Most leaders continue to adhere to the old unwritten rule that admonishes them to cover up errors and hide mistakes.

The tendency is to move from crisis to crisis, hardly stopping to see what went wrong. This leads to denial and causes us to look away from errors, rather than toward them—kind of like a golfer who hits a bad drive and doesn't want to watch as it heads for the woods.

A few forward-thinking companies have learned to celebrate mistakes as opportunities for learning. I know of a large organization that shoots off a cannon when a big mistake is made. The leaders are not saying they enjoy making errors; they're saying it's time for everyone to learn something. Other organizations would do well to adopt a similar policy. After all, how can they improve if they don't learn from their mistakes?

Choose work you love and you will never have to work a day in your life.

—Confucius

For most people, there's a big difference between work and play. Work is something you have to do; play is something you choose to do. I believe you have a great job if you can't tell the difference, and the best leaders are those who absolutely love what they're doing.

Don Shula was a great football coach because there was nothing he'd rather do on a Sunday than coach his team toward victory.

To ensure that your work is also your play, I recommend that you develop a personal mission statement. This will help you find what it is you enjoy so much that you lose track of time while doing it. That's a difficult concept for some people. But why shouldn't life be about doing what you love? If you don't enjoy what you're doing, how can you be really good at it?

We should all be saying, "Thank God it's Monday!"

Winning coaches make their teams audible-ready.

—Ken Blanchard and Don Shula
Everyone's a Coach

An *audible* is a football term—a verbal command used to alert the players to substitute new assignments for the ones they were prepared to perform. Suppose, for example, that the quarterback goes to the line of scrimmage and realizes that the defense has figured out their strategy and is ready to stop them. Does he follow through with the doomed play? Of course not. He signals for a different play that has a better chance of success. An audible allows the quarterback to do what makes sense.

Audibles are not just last-minute orders the quarterback has dreamed up out of nowhere. These are strategies the players know about and have practiced. There is nothing wrong with having plans, or policies, or rules. The problem comes when people are told to implement them no matter what.

I get frustrated with people who tell customers, "Sorry, that's our policy," even when the policy doesn't make sense. Teach your people to bring their brains to work and to be "audible-ready."

People are OK; it's their behavior that's a problem sometimes.

—Ken Blanchard and Spencer Johnson
The One Minute Manager

What's the best response when one of your people makes a mistake? First of all, check out the facts. If the person admits to making the mistake and corrects it, you're off the hook. If not, I recommend the One Minute Reprimand.

Tell the person involved exactly what he or she did wrong and explain how it impacted the team or organization. Next, share with the person how you feel about it—"I'm frustrated and disappointed with what happened." Pause for a moment to let your remarks sink in, and then reaffirm your confidence in the individual.

People sometimes ask, "Why reaffirm someone you're upset with?" Reaffirming is important because you want the person to walk away thinking about correcting the wrong behavior, rather than how he or she has been mistreated or misunderstood. You want to get rid of the behavior, not the person.

Consistency isn't behaving
the same way all the time.

—Ken Blanchard and Don Shula
Everyone's a Coach

Consistency does not mean behaving the same way all the time. It actually means behaving the same way under similar circumstances. I believe in praising people, but I also know that if you praise them when they are performing well *and* when they are performing poorly, you are sending them an inconsistent message. Good performance should always be treated differently than poor performance.

Many leaders make the mistake of letting their mood determine how they respond to their people. If they're feeling great, they wander around praising everyone. If they're feeling lousy, they wander around pointing out what everyone is doing wrong.

When you respond to your people in the same way under similar circumstances, you give them a valuable gift: the gift of predictability. There are many ways to inspire good performance, but what maintains and improves it is responding in a consistent manner.

This is the first time in the history of business that you can be great at what you're doing today and be out of business tomorrow.

—Ken Blanchard and Terry Waghorn
Mission Possible

Constant change is a way of life in business today. In fact, to stay competitive, you must simultaneously manage the present and plan for the future.

The problem is that you can't have the same people doing both jobs. If people with present-time operational responsibilities are asked to think about the future, they will kill it. If people with responsibilities for the future also have present-time duties, the urgent problems of today will drag them away from tomorrow's opportunities.

My wife, Margie, stepped down as president of our company to become director of the Office of the Future. She has a four-member team, which has been freed from present-time responsibilities in order to focus all its attention on future trends and technology changes in our industry. The team proposes any changes they see that need to be made to the board of directors. The board weighs the merits of the proposal and decides whether to pass it on to the present-time leaders. Once a future sighting is turned over to the present-time leaders, the Office of the Future lets go of it.

The only job security you
have today is your
commitment to
continuous personal
improvement.

When I graduated from college, a friend of mine got a job with AT&T. He called home to tell his mother, and she cried, "You're set for life!" Would you be set for life with AT&T today? Of course not, and neither are you set for life with any other organization. The "old deal" (loyalty in exchange for job security) is over.

In searching for the "new deal," I've asked people all over the world, "If you can't have job security, what do you want from an organization?" First of all, they want honesty. Second, they want the opportunity to learn new skills. If they have to look for a new job, internally or externally, they want to be able to compete.

Once you realize the reality of the "new deal," you must make up your mind to control your circumstances by means of continuous personal improvement. The sign on your bathroom mirror should say, "Getting better all the time."

When you know what you
stand for, you can turn
around on a dime and
have five cents change.

Ask yourself how long it would take your people to process a major product change, get behind it, and still meet deadlines. The key to having an outstanding, enthusiastic, flexible, and on-time team is to make sure your people are values-driven, rather than goals-driven. If the number-one shared value is to serve the customer, then they will be ready to do whatever it takes to live that value.

In our book *Gung Ho!,* Sheldon Bowles and I make an important distinction between values and goals. The minute you proclaim a goal, it's real and it's set. Values don't work that way. Values become real only when you demonstrate them in the way you act and the way you insist others behave. Goals are for the future; values are for now. Goals are set; values are lived. Goals change; values are rocks you can count on.

Share the cash, then share
the congratulations.

—Ken Blanchard and Sheldon Bowles
Gung Ho!

You can pat your people on the back and congratulate them all you want, but if you're not taking care of their need for cash, your praise won't ring true.

I was working with a major retail chain that was experiencing an annual turnover rate of more than 100 percent. The odd thing was that an up-to-date employee opinion survey showed that the workers liked the company, approved of the way they were being managed, and appreciated the upbeat environment.

"Why are they leaving when we get such positive feedback?" the chairman asked me.

"Did you notice that the lowest ranked survey item was pay and benefits?" I asked. "People are leaving because their basic needs are not being met."

A large segment of our U.S. population is hurting financially. So remember, if you want to build credibility, follow this rule: first cash, then congratulations.

There is no pillow as soft as
a clear conscience.

—John Wooden
former UCLA head basketball coach
and Hall of Fame member

In today's competitive environment, some leaders are tempted to abandon ethical considerations. Somehow they think they can win by playing by the rule of "anything goes."

These leaders are jeopardizing far more than they imagine. First, they stand to lose respect. The number-one characteristic employees say they are looking for in a leader is integrity. They also risk losing repeat customers and competent people. You can make a quick financial gain by taking advantage of your customers or your people, but the loss of trust may never be restored. The third thing they are placing at risk is their own self-esteem.

Yes, self-esteem! Meeting people with a clear conscience puts you at ease and allows you to concentrate on doing your best work. When you deal straight with people, they sense they can trust you. And when you lie down at night, your clear conscience makes a wonderfully soft pillow.

It's surprising how much
you can accomplish if
you don't care who
gets the credit.

—Abraham Lincoln

It is healthy and justifiable to feel good about your accomplishments. That's what true pride is all about. But there is a false pride that distorts people's images of their own importance. They think they deserve all the credit, are the source of all ideas, and their work is the most important. Nothing can get leaders off track more quickly than a big head and false pride.

Sharing credit is all about self-esteem. People who have to get all the credit and act like they are the only ones who count are actually covering up their own "I-don't-count" feelings.

Suppose tomorrow a lightening bolt strikes you and increases your self-esteem by 100 percent. Would you act differently? Sure you would. Would you be willing to share credit with your people? Of course. Would they perform better as a result? You had better believe it. Let's hope for some lightning bolts!

Positive thinkers get
positive results because
they are not afraid
of problems.

—Ken Blanchard and Norman Vincent Peale
The Power of Ethical Management

The minute you mention the word *problem*, the implication is that you are speaking negatively. But some don't see it that way.

People often asked Norman Vincent Peale, "Don't you think life would be better if we had fewer problems?"

Norman would answer that question by saying, "I'll be happy to take you to Woodlawn Cemetery because the only people I know who don't have any problems are dead."

Norman thought it was possible that the more problems you have, the more alive you are. "If you have no problems at all," he would say, "you're in grave jeopardy!" In fact, if you really insisted that you had no problems, he would suggest that you immediately race home, go straight to your bedroom and slam the door. Then get down on your knees and pray, "What's the matter, Lord? Don't You trust me anymore? Give me some problems!"

Early in life, people give
up their health to gain
wealth.… In later life,
people give up some
of their wealth to
regain health!

—Ken Blanchard, D. W. Edington, and Marjorie Blanchard
The One Minute Manager Balances Work and Life

If you don't watch out, success can kill you. When *The One Minute Manager* leaped onto the best-seller list, I found myself running around the country giving speeches, conducting interviews on radio and television—doing all the things that seem to come with material success.

One day I looked at myself and realized I was overweight, out of shape, sleep deprived, and generally treating my body like it was indestructible. My wife, Margie, began telling me I needed to get my life in balance. Finally, I took the advice of my wife and friends and began to develop a sensible lifestyle program. It was then that Dee Edington, Margie, and I began writing *The One Minute Manager Balances Work and Life* (formerly *The One Minute Manager Gets Fit*). By the time the book came off the press, I was the picture of health.

The reality was that I needed that book more than anyone else. I had to give up some of my wealth to regain my health. What are you doing to keep your life balanced?

Servant leadership is more about character than style.

I n his book *Servant Leadership,* Robert Greenleaf defines two kinds of leaders. Strong natural leaders are those who try to take control, make the decisions, and give the orders in any situation in which they find themselves; they have a need to be in charge. Strong natural servants, on the other hand, will assume leadership only if they see it as a way in which they can serve.

You would think that natural leaders would use a directive, autocratic style, while natural servants would use a more supportive, participative style. This assumption falls short because it confuses style with character.

I want to be led by strong natural servants because they are willing to use whatever leadership style—directive, supportive, or some combination—that best serves the needs of those they are leading. Remember that the primary biblical image of servant leadership is that of the shepherd. The flock is not there for the sake of the shepherd; the shepherd is there for the sake of the flock.

Am I a servant leader or a self-serving leader?

—Ken Blanchard and Phil Hodges
The Servant Leader

This question, when answered with brutal honesty, will go to the core of your intention or motivation as a leader.

One of the quickest ways you can tell the difference between servant leaders and self-serving leaders is how they handle feedback, since one of the biggest fears that self-serving leaders have is losing their position. Self-serving leaders spend most of their time protecting their status. If you give them feedback, how do they usually respond? Negatively. They think your feedback means you don't want their leadership anymore.

Servant leaders, however, look at leadership as an act of service. They embrace and welcome feedback, viewing it as a source of useful information on how they can provide better service.

Ducks quack.

Eagles soar.

Years ago, writer and motivational speaker Wayne Dyer said, "There are two kinds of people in this world: ducks and eagles." Ducks quack a lot and make all kinds of noise. Eagles go about their business and soar above the crowd. When a customer problem arises, you can tell a lot about an organization. This is usually when ducks and eagles appear.

Eagles flourish in organizations where the customer is the focus, while ducks multiply in places where boss pleasing and policy following carry the day. Let me give you an example.

I once tried to rent a car in Ithaca, New York. I planned to fly out of Syracuse, so I asked for a car from Syracuse in order to avoid the drop-off fee. The clerk located a car from Syracuse, but the $50 fee remained on my contract. "I can't take it off; my computer won't let me, and my boss would kill me," she quacked. It took me twenty minutes to get this woman to remove the drop-off fee. What kind of organization do you think she works for?

Eagles flourish when
they're free to fly.

I was greeted the minute I walked into the Department of Motor Vehicles to replace my lost driver's license. "Welcome. Do you speak English or Spanish?" an employee asked. She then ushered me to a counter where a smiling young man asked how he could help me. Nine minutes later, I had a temporary license.

"This isn't the DMV I used to know and love," I commented. "What happened?"

"Haven't you met our manager?" the employee asked, pointing at a desk smack in the middle of the big room. I walked over to meet "the boss" and found him to be anything but. He told me that it was his job "to reorganize the department on a moment-by-moment basis, depending on customer needs." His commitment to taking care of citizens was obvious.

Duck busting was that manager's way of life. He wanted eagles that would create Raving Fan customers. I certainly went away as one.

Take responsibility for
making relationships work.

L et me ask you a question—the same question you should be asking yourself, not only about your love relationship, but also your relationship with your children, your boss, your coworkers, your direct reports, and your friends. Do you want the relationship to work? If so, then you must take personal responsibility for making it work. And forget the word *trying*. Trying is just a noisy way of not doing something.

I know a couple who has been married for twenty-five years. The two partners are an inspiration to others. They seem to be courting each other all the time. Whenever they see each other, both light up with joy. It's obvious that they're best friends. Though it's easy to accentuate the negative, these two do everything they can to point out the positive and bring out the best in each other. They are both committed to doing whatever it takes to show respect and unconditional appreciation.

In short, they are committed to making their relationship work. That's what it takes these days in all types of relationships.

New today,
obsolete tomorrow.

I t used to be that managers were the people who were the best at doing the jobs of the people they were supervising. But changes happen so quickly today that it's almost impossible to be a "know-it-all" anymore. These days, within a year, most managers know far less than their people about the jobs their doing. Not admitting this can lead to real problems. Yet traditionally, managers have not been willing to share their vulnerability.

One of the most ingratiating things you can do with your people is to admit your ignorance or vulnerability. Once done, this opens the door for others to share their vulnerabilities too.

We're all sometimes confused, lost, or afraid. If we come clean about these insecurities, we create trust and empower others to learn and grow. So if you're obsolete, who cares? Someone around you will have the answer, and your ignorance will allow that person to shine.

G.O.L.F. stands for Game of Life First.

—Ken Blanchard
The One Minute Golfer
(formerly *Playing the Great Game of Golf*)

I've often said I can find out more about people during one round of golf than by working with them for a long period of time. Like life, golf is a game in which you get some good breaks and bad breaks you don't deserve—and some good breaks and bad breaks you *do* deserve.

In most sports, you are reacting to someone else, but in golf you are reacting to your own performance. Sometimes you are playing better than you expect and dealing with success; sometimes you are playing worse than you expect and dealing with failure.

Golf brings out the best and worst in people. If you cheat or blow up when you have a bad break, that same behavior will show up in other parts of your life. If you maintain a positive attitude when things go sour, this will carry over into other aspects of your life as well. What better training ground is there for learning to accept the bitter with the sweet than the golf course? Go ahead—tee it up!

Leadership is not something you do to people. It's something you do with people.

—Ken Blanchard, Patricia Zigarmi, and Drea Zigarmi
Leadership and The One Minute Manager

When we first started teaching Situational Leadership® II, we found that leaders got excited about it and started using the concepts with their people. The only problem was they didn't tell anybody. As a result, people got confused, even when they were using the concepts well.

For example, suppose you have found some of your people to be self-reliant achievers. Because you feel they can work well with little supervision, you stop going by to see them. Suppose also that you have several enthusiastic beginners who need to be told how and why they should do things. The achievers might feel undervalued and overlooked, while the beginners could feel you are picking on them.

When you share your leadership strategy with your people, they not only understand what you have in mind, but they can give you helpful feedback. True servant leaders want feedback because they are anxious to know whether their interactions with their people are helpful and effective. So don't do leadership *to* people—do it *with* them.

Don't settle for less than a
Fortunate 500 company.

—Ken Blanchard and Michael O'Connor
Managing by Values

What is a Fortunate 500 company? It's an organization that has motivated customers who keep coming back; inspired people who give their best each day; owners who enjoy profits made in an ethically fair manner; and significant others (suppliers, community, vendors, distributors, and even respected competitors) who thrive on the mutual trust and respect they feel toward the company.

How do you get relationships like that? It's the result of MBV—managing by values. There are three MBV steps: identifying core values, communicating core values, and aligning values and practice. All are important.

Take time to identify
core values.

I dentifying the core values that define your organization is one of the most important functions of leadership. The success or failure of this process can literally make or break an organization.

For example, let's look at The Walt Disney Company. This organization has identified four values for its theme parks: safety, courtesy, the show (being in role, whether it's being Mickey Mouse or a ticket taker), and efficiency. Not only has it identified its values, but is has also carefully ordered them. Why is this important? A bottom-line-oriented manager might emphasize efficiency and thus jeopardize the other three values.

You would be wise to make the identification of your organization's core values a top priority. And don't try to do this job alone. Take advantage of the resources you have around you and bring everyone into the process early. Draw in your people—everyone should have ownership in this process. Remember that rules can be imposed, but values cannot.

Core values must be communicated.

—Ken Blanchard and Jesse Stoner
Full Steam Ahead!

I dentifying your organization's core values is a worthless exercise unless those values are constantly communicated, and your people and customers see that you are completely committed to them.

In fact, it's impossible to affirm your core values too much. Talk about them; put them on your business cards, annual reports, plaques, wall signs, and job aids. In short, display these values anywhere your people, customers, stockholders, and significant others can see them.

Max Duprec, the legendary retired chairman of Herman Miller, used to say that when it came to sharing vision and values, he had to be like a third grade teacher: He had to repeat them over and over and over again until people got it right, right, right.

You must give more than lip service to these values. However, lip service is an important step in the process. Stating and restating them until they become second nature breeds security for your people and your customers alike. They will begin to know what to expect from your organization, and that kind of recognition will set you apart from the crowd.

Walk your talk.

Without some method of locating gaps between values and behavior, identifying and communicating core values will do more harm than good. For example, an organization that talks about putting the customer first, but fails to do so is far more likely to be judged harshly by its people and customers alike.

This means that it is vital for organizations and their leaderships to "walk their talk." They must make every effort to become living symbols of their organization's value system. This is simple common sense. Eighty percent of the time allocated for implementing the "managing by values" process is given to this step. Why? Because without it, the other steps are useless.

The good news is that once core values have been set in place—identified, communicated, and impacting behavior—they become the "boss." And keep in mind this is an ongoing process, a journey without a finish line.

Embody the values.

—Ken Blanchard and Mark Miller
The Secret

All genuine leadership is built on trust—and there are many ways to build trust. One way is to live consistently with the values you profess. For example, if you say customers are important, your actions had better support that statement. If you choose to live as if customers aren't important, people will have reason to question your trustworthiness. And in the final analysis, if you are deemed untrustworthy by people, you will not be trusted—or followed—as a leader.

To be successful as a leader, you must know the values of your organization and live by them. You've got to walk the talk. Don't be like so many leaders who stumble the mumble by saying one thing and doing another. When you embody the values you profess, you become the kind of leader that others gladly follow.

Knowing where you're going is the first step to getting there.

—Ken Blanchard
We Are the Beloved

Have you identified your mission in life—your reason for being? Establishing a personal mission statement is an important exercise that has helped me define who I am, identify my passions and priorities, and keep my perspective on target.

I've noticed that I'm happiest and at my best when I'm teaching or writing. I also want to make a difference in other people's lives. Therefore, my mission statement reads, "To be a loving teacher and example of simple truths that help myself and others to awaken the presence of God in our lives." I say, "awaken the presence of God" because I am constantly encouraging myself and others to get our egos out of the way so God can do His work. Remember: *ego* really stands for "edging God out."

Look inside yourself and let God help you find the driving force in your life. Doing so is the first step to a happier and more satisfied you.

As a leader, the most important earthly relationship you can cultivate is your relationship with yourself.

—Ken Blanchard and Terry Waghorn
Mission Possible

D o you really know yourself? Do you have a personal "mission statement" that defines your strengths and motivates you to be all God meant you to be?

If you have trouble with that question, you might want to try an interesting activity that will almost certainly help you develop a clearer sense of purpose and personal identity: Write your own obituary.

I know it sounds strange—even a little morbid. But this exercise is not about dying; it's about living. It will give you an opportunity to adjust your life, describe the ideal you, and define what it is you would like to be remembered for. Why leave such important matters to chance? God has a wonderful plan for your life. Let Him help you establish your path and guide you as you walk in it. Nothing will be beyond your reach.

Purpose can never be
about achievement;
it is much bigger.

—Ken Blanchard and Terry Waghorn
Mission Possible

The beauty of writing your own obituary before you die is that it serves as a dream—a big picture of what you want your life to be and mean. So, if you don't like the way your life is shaping up right now, change it. Don't hold back!

Put aside your lesser self and go with your best self. This will probably require some personal meditation, but it will pay big dividends. And reject the lie that says such thinking is egotistical. God made you, and He has always intended for you to be the best that you can be. He not only approves, but I have found that He is willing and able to help in your search for self-discovery. Quiet yourself, pray, and listen to the voice that says, "You are loved, richly and unconditionally."

And as you begin, remember that every journey begins with a single step and moves along one step at a time. Enjoy the trip!

Purpose has to do with
one's calling—deciding
what business you are
in as a person.

—Ken Blanchard and Norman Vincent Peale
The Power of Ethical Management

I once heard a story about Alfred Nobel, the originator of the Nobel Peace Prize. When his brother died, Nobel got a copy of the newspaper to see what was said about his brother. He was shocked to discover that a dreadful error had been made: The paper had confused him with his brother, and the obituary he was reading was his own.

As a young man, Alfred Nobel had been involved in the invention of dynamite, and his premature obituary elaborated on the terrible death and destruction this powerful force had brought into the world. Nobel was devastated. He wanted to be known as a man of peace. He quickly realized that if his obituary were to be rewritten, he would have to do it himself by changing the nature of his life. So Alfred Nobel did just that. I dare say that Alfred Nobel is better known today for his contribution to peace rather than any other thing he did in his life.

Your life is yours to design. Make it all it can be!

ABOUT THE AUTHOR

Ken Blanchard has had an extraordinary impact on the day-to-day management of millions of people and companies. He is the author of more than forty books, including the blockbuster international best seller *The One Minute Manager* and the giant business best sellers *Leadership and the One Minute Manager*, *Raving Fans*, and *Gung Ho!* His books have combined sales of more than eighteen million copies in more than twenty-five languages. In 2005 Ken was inducted into Amazon's Hall of Fame as one of the top twenty-five best-selling authors of all time.

Ken is the chief spiritual officer of The Ken Blanchard Companies, an international management training and consulting firm that he and his wife, Dr. Marjorie Blanchard, founded in 1979. He is also cofounder of the Lead Like Jesus Ministries, a nonprofit organization dedicated to inspiring and equipping people to be servant leaders in the marketplace. He is a visiting lecturer at his alma mater, Cornell University, where he received his bachelor's and PhD degrees and is a trustee emeritus of the board of trustees.

SERVICES AVAILABLE

For more than twenty-eight years, The Ken Blanchard Companies has been in the business of helping leaders and organizations lead at a higher level. An award-winning provider of corporate training, the company is a global leader in workplace learning, productivity, performance, and leadership effectiveness. It is best known for its Situational Leadership® II program, the most widely taught leadership model in the world.

Based on the belief that people are the key to accomplishing strategic objectives and driving business results, Blanchard programs develop excellence in leadership, teams, customer loyalty, change management, and performance improvement. By showing people how to make the shift from learning to doing, Blanchard consulting partners have helped clients in more than fifty countries achieve their business strategies. These partners are available for training initiatives, consulting engagements, and keynote addresses around the world.

Global Headquarters
The Ken Blanchard Companies
125 State Place
Escondido, CA 92029
www.kenblanchard.com
+1.800.728.6000 from the United States
+1.760.489.5005 from anywhere

BIBLIOGRAPHY

The One Minute Manager® with Spencer Johnson, 1981

Leadership and the One Minute Manager® with Patricia Zigarmi and Drea Zigarmi, 1985

The Power of Ethical Management with Norman Vincent Peale, 1988

The One Minute Manager® Meets the Monkey with William Oncken and Hal Burrows, 1989

The One Minute Manager® Builds High Performing Teams with Don Carew and Eunice Parisi-Carew, 1990

Raving Fans® with Sheldon Bowles, 1993

Everyone's a Coach with Don Shula, 1995

Gung Ho! with Sheldon Bowles, 1998

High Five! with Sheldon Bowles, Don Carew and Eunice Parisi-Carew, 2001

Whale Done!™ with Thad Lacinak, Chuck Tompkins and Jim Ballard, 2002

The Servant Leader with Phil Hodges, 2003

Full Steam Ahead! with Jesse Stoner, 2003

The Secret with Mark Miller, 2004

Leading at a Higher Level with the Founding Associates and Consulting Partners of The Ken Blanchard Companies, 2006